*Far View Ruin, with snow-capped
La Plata Mountains in the background*

View from Point Lookout, near Park Entrance

MESA VERDE

NATIONAL PARK

PRESERVING THE PAST

BY ROBERT H. LISTER AND FLORENCE C. LISTER

Produced by Sequoia Communications
2020 Alameda Padre Serra, Santa Barbara, CA 93103
Edited by Janie Freeburg
Copyedited by Mark Schlenz
Designed by Gay Hagen
Printed in Japan
ISBN 0-917859-13-8
Library of Congress No. 86-063917

ACKNOWLEDGMENTS

Our sincere appreciation is extended to the following people whose efforts made this book possible: Mesa Verde National Park Superintendent Robert C. Heyder; Chief Park Interpreter Donald C. Fiero; District Interpreter Linda A. Martin; photographer A. William Kreutz; authors Robert H. Lister and Florence C. Lister; Anne Markward and the employees of the National Park Service and ARA Mesa Verde who make this Park so enjoyable for others.

Bruce W. Fears
ARA Mesa Verde Company

PHOTOGRAPHY & ART

Horace M. Albright Collection: 27. *ARA Mesa Verde Company:* inside back cover, left and lower right. *Judd Cooney:* 56; 73; 79 inset. *Joe Cummins:* Back Flap, bottom; inside front cover; 5 top left, lower left and lower right; 37 top; 42; 46; 51; 74-75; 76. *Victor Goodwin:* back cover; 8; 12; 13; 24; 52; 54; 57; 60; 61; 66 left; 67; 79. *Karen Hayes:* 20-21; 28; 72. *Jerry Jacka:* front flap; 4; 16; 35 bottom; 36-37; 36 inset; 40-41; 43; 44-45; 47 right; 48; 49; 58-9; 61; 70. *C. Allan Morgan:* 33; 65; 77; 78. *Jeff Nicholas:* 25; 71. *National Park Service* (copy photography by William Creutz) back flap top; 10; 11; 14; 15; 18; 19; 21 inset; 22; 23; 26; 29; 30; 34; 35 top; 39. *Laura Thomas:* 47 left; 50; 66 right; 68-69. *Dave Wappler:* cover; title page; 6-7; 60; inside back cover top right. Illustrations by Frank Becker: 32, 38, 59. Pictorial map by Oceana Maps: 80.

Anasazi ruins frame the clear Colorado skies.

CONTENTS

"Those who cannot remember the past are condemned to repeat it."
—George Santayana

CHAPTER I

WHO WERE THE MESA VERDIANS?

Around 11,000 B.C. the ancestors of the Mesa Verdians entered the Southwest. Originating in northeastern Asia, they had crossed the Bering Straits land bridge into North America and wandered for unknown generations in a southerly route through glacier-free corridors of the new continent.

These immigrants were lured by large herds of mammoth, bison, camels and horses upon which they fed. Dwarfed in size and brute strength by their prey, these Paleo-Indians had the incalculable advantage of brain power. Wooden spears with stone points attached were propelled with bone shattering force by a leverage-enhancing thrower, or *atlatl*. To this weaponry Paleo-Indians added the impact of their own numbers and the element of surprise. They also exploited natural topographic and climatic features. Animals could be driven over abrupt precipices or into snow drifts or bogs from which they could not escape. Survival consumed all the energies of Paleo-Indians in the New World. They left little evidence behind other than some widely dispersed stone points, knives or scrapers.

As northern ice sheets receded, conditions to the south became warmer and drier. The grasslands shrank, many water sources evaporated, and by about 4000 B.C. most of the large Ice Age mammals were extinct or had moved eastward. Some hunters followed them on to the wide interior plains. To survive,

Corrugated pottery jar, found in Long House.

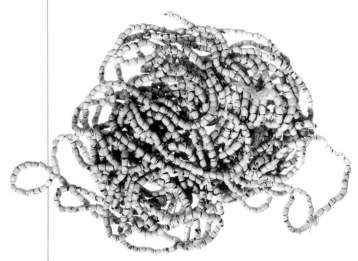

Shell beads, part of the Anasazi trading wealth.
Preceding page: Spruce Tree House.

those who remained in what was becoming the desert Southwest were forced into a close symbiosis with their altered environment. Adapting to the widely varied ecosystems of the region, they shifted from a red meat based diet to an omnivorous one in which meat was a secondary element. A wide selection of edible wild plants was augmented by small game such as deer, bighorn sheep, antelope and rodents. New stone grinding implements for processing vegetable materials were developed. New types of game required stone projectile points smaller than those needed to bring down the huge animals of former times. Life was a continual foraging for the green shoots, cactus leaves and fruits of springtime or the maturing seeds and nuts of fall. The bands travelled back and forth across a swath of terrain encompassing mountains, plateaus and deserts.

Around 1,000 B.C. people of the Southwest began experimenting in growing a primitive form of corn. This important food crop was domesticated farther south at least three thousand years earlier from a wild tropical grass native to central Mexico. Over five centuries, strains of the early small-cobbed corn were adapted to various microenvironments of the Southwest, and bred selectively into plants yielding larger kernels. In the same period, squash and beans, also from Mexico, appeared in the Southwest. After about 400 B.C., as the agricultural revolution took hold, this triad of domesticated plants—corn, beans, squash—became the dietary mainstay of most Southwesterners. These highly nutritious foods could be dried and stored for long periods. In good times the hunting of small animals and the gathering of native plants became less important. This development brought a new security.

When sole dependence upon hunting and gathering gave way to horticulture a more advanced culture was reached. In what archeologists call "the Southwest Tradition," the new focus was small-scale farming with fixed residency, though full use of all natural resources remained important. Small kinship groups established simple shelters fashioned from materials at hand. They began to store whatever meager food surpluses could be accumulated during ripening seasons to carry them through the barren months. Life expanded to a vision of tomorrow—as well as of today.

Rock art at Mesa Verde's Petroglyph Point.

The Southwest Tradition, with its reliance upon food production, slowly crystallized as early as 500-300 B.C. along the southern portions of New Mexico and Arizona, areas closest to the Mexican cultural hearth. Farming gradually spread northward, until at higher elevations, with colder climates and shorter growing seasons, the development of new varieties of corn was required. It was not until around A.D. 500 that the tradition was well established over most of Arizona, western New Mexico, and the southern parts of Utah and Colorado.

Extensive archaeological investigation had traced the thousand-year prehistoric progression of the Southwest Tradition through three stages. First (300/100 B.C. to A.D. 500/700), there were scattered small *hamlets* of flimsy pithouses. Life included the use of simple red or brown pottery vessels, and a carry-over of many basic artifacts and practices from earlier times.

Second (A.D. 500/700 to 1000/1100), there followed a stage marked by territorial expansion, improved farming methods, and *villages* with both semisubterranean and surface houses. Villages featured storage units and structures used specifically for ceremonial purposes. New pottery forms and decorative styles were developed, and there were marked changes in religious, social and economic practices. Cultural peaks were enjoyed in some localities during this time.

The third stage (A.D. 1000/1100 to 1450/1600) was characterized by *towns,* a result of increased population, the drawing together

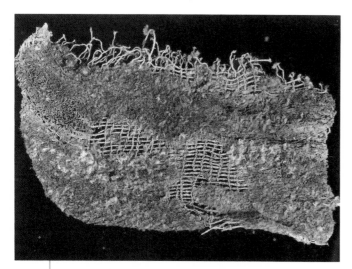

Fragment of a woven feather robe.

A carefully decorated water jug.

A woven yucca-fiber pillow. Opposite: the north portion of Mug House, before excavation.

Southwest Tradition. They harassed and raided the town dwellers for foodstuffs, commodities and slaves.

Archaeologists detect three contemporaneous major cultural groups within the overall Southwest Tradition that reflect adaptations to distinctive environmental zones. The desert adjacent to the Gila and Salt river networks of southern Arizona supported *the Hohokam,* a subculture rich in artists and craftsmen, skilled in irrigation agriculture, who were active in exporting and consuming trade commodities exchanged with other Southwesterners and Mexican entrepreneurs.

The *Mogollon* subculture, found in the mountains and basins straddling the borders between southern New Mexico and Arizona and between those states and Mexico, was slow to advance beyond the hamlet and village stages. The Mogollones lagged behind their neighbors in architecture, most arts and crafts, and technology.

To the north the *Anasazi* ("ancient ones"), concentrated on the high, starkly beautiful country of the Colorado Plateau, were responsible for developments that resulted in the most spectacular ruins in the Southwest. They integrated architectural and engineering skills, adequate building materials and a lot of well-directed human energy into becoming the master builders of the Southwest. High quality pottery, characteristically exhibiting black designs on white backgrounds, was another achievement of the Anasazi. Their farming relied upon rainfall or directing runoff water onto garden plots. Trade was widespread, and a few centers existed where local turquoise and exotic items of shell, copper and feathers seem to have been assembled and redistributed. Foreign imports came from Mexico, along with construction and communication ideas. Religious ceremonialism was a highly developed, integral part of everyday life. Ritual specialists are thought to have led group participants in annual cycles or ceremonies timed, in part, by astronomical observations.

At their zenith, the aggressive Anasazi extended their sphere of influence south into the territories of both the Mogollon and Hohokam. Mesa Verde National Park, known for its beautiful "cliff cities," is a striking example of the Anasazi legacy.

CHAPTER II

UNCOVERING MESA VERDE'S SECRETS

DISCOVERIES, ARCHAEOLOGY AND PRESERVATION

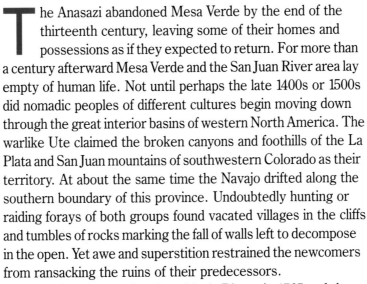

The Anasazi abandoned Mesa Verde by the end of the thirteenth century, leaving some of their homes and possessions as if they expected to return. For more than a century afterward Mesa Verde and the San Juan River area lay empty of human life. Not until perhaps the late 1400s or 1500s did nomadic peoples of different cultures begin moving down through the great interior basins of western North America. The warlike Ute claimed the broken canyons and foothills of the La Plata and San Juan mountains of southwestern Colorado as their territory. At about the same time the Navajo drifted along the southern boundary of this province. Undoubtedly hunting or raiding forays of both groups found vacated villages in the cliffs and tumbles of rocks marking the fall of walls left to decompose in the open. Yet awe and superstition restrained the newcomers from ransacking the ruins of their predecessors.

Two Spanish parties, Juan Maria Rivera in 1765 and the black-robed friars Sylvestre Velez de Escalante and Francisco Atanasia Dominguez in 1776, are believed to have marched along the outer skirts of the Mesa Verde prominence. They proceeded on their journeys without bothering to explore the flat topped plateau, though Rivera may have named it.

In 1859 geologist John S. Newberry climbed the mesa escarpment, enjoyed the view, and descended without suspecting the sleeping antiquities nearby. He was followed fifteen years later by three men rewarded with the first sightings of Mesa Verde ruins, though it is certain that occasional, less literate, wanderers had seen them earlier. William Henry Jackson, photographer for the U.S. Geological and Geographical Survey of the

The Wetherill Brothers. Seated, left to right: Alfred, Richard, John; standing: Win and Clayton. Preceding page: Cliff Palace.

Territories, and biologist Ernest Ingersoll climbed into Two Story House in Mancos Canyon in 1874, having previously seen other scatters of small ruins along their route. The next year geologist William H. Holmes found Sixteen Window House, also in Mancos Canyon, and took two pottery vessels from it.

In 1886 Virginia Donague, a young New York journalist, led a party back down Mancos Canyon, noting two minor Anasazi structures in lower tributaries and the most sizeable cliff dwelling thus far found: Brown Stone Front House, now called Balcony House. The cliff dwellings so inspired Miss Donague that, under her married name of Mrs. Gilbert McClurg, she became a leader of a ladies' group lobbying to have the area around the ruins set aside as a national preserve.

THE WETHERILLS

Meanwhile, virgin land surrounding the Mesa Verde was being reclaimed by homesteaders and ranchers who commonly encountered in their fields heaps of rock that had once been room walls. The quest for "relics" became a regional pastime. What was not realized at the time was that they had come to an area that once contained some of the densest prehistoric population north of central Mexico.

Among the incoming settlers was the Wetherill family, boasting five grown sons and a daughter, who developed a ranch in the verdant Mancos Valley. They were as intrigued as their neighbors by the possibility of antiquities at their doorstep. The Wetherills unknowingly had greater chance of discovery than most, having obtained permission from the Utes to winter cattle on Indian lands which at that time encompassed most of the Mesa Verde. According to local folklore, on two days in mid-December, 1888, Cliff Palace, Spruce Tree House and Square Tower House were seen for the first time by white men.

With these major cliff dwellings and Balcony House known, the Mesa Verde ruins rush was on. For a short time the sites were mined with the same fervor as the Mother Lode. The aim was to take advantage of a potential resource, the store of cast-aside artifacts the Anasazi had left behind. Within four years, 182 cliff ruins had been probed, and three large collections of artifacts—predominantly pottery vessels—had been sold, eventually reaching the vaults of the Colorado State Historical Society, the University of Pennsylvania Museum and the Colorado State Museum.

As word spread about the fabulous finds at Mesa Verde, the Wetherills guided others to this shrine of prehistory. Among these first visitors was Frederick H. Chapin, for whom the mesa which was most intensively occupied by the Mesa Verdians was later named.

Fortunately just three years after Cliff Palace was found a young Swede turned up at the Wetherill's Alamo Ranch wanting to be

Balcony House as seen by the Wetherills. John Wetherill is seated among the ruins.

taken to the Mesa Verde ruins. He was Gustaf Nordenskïold, well-educated elder son of a famous arctic explorer. Nordenskïold's planned week-long stay extended into several months, during which he explored twenty-seven principal sites, excavating and collecting specimens. It was he who named one of the areas in which he worked "Wetherill's Mesa." Nordenskïold kept meticulous field notes and made maps and photographs as his work progressed. Because there were then no laws preventing export of antiquities, the Nordenskïold collection was sent to Stockholm, and ultimately to the National Museum of Finland. The results of Nordenskïold's extensive study of Mesa Verde cliff dwellings were published in 1893. From that time on, research increasingly replaced undocumented exploitation.

MESA VERDE IS PRESERVED AS A NATIONAL PARK

After years of agitation by local citizens deploring vandalism of the ruins, Mesa Verde National Park was created in 1906 during the administration of President Theodore Roosevelt. It remains the only federal park dedicated to the works of prehistoric man. A two-season survey of the most important cliff

sites on the sides of Chapin and Wetherill mesas followed to determine the quantity and quality of the archaeological resources that had been included in the nation's legacy. Photographs taken at the time provide an historical data base for the appearance of the ruins when first visited. From 1908 through 1922, excluding the World War I years, sixteen of the largest cliff dwellings were made ready for public visitation. Two mesa top sites were excavated to provide some information about earlier stages of the evolving sedentary culture not apparent in the large remains. The last unlooted cliff dwelling, Daniels House, was entered in 1915. It yielded

A partially-excavated jar at Cliff Palace.

a dozen large earthenware pots, several stone axes, and other small objects that had been left where last used some six hundred years earlier.

While this initial work was going on at Mesa Verde, numerous other prehistoric remains were being found and excavated across the Colorado Plateau. It was becoming apparent that from the craggy red lands of the Kayenta district in northwest Arizona, to bleak Chaco Canyon south of the San Juan, to the Galisteo basin east of the Rio Grande, there had been a basic common culture. It was time to become familiar with the range of these antiquities and salvage as much from them as possible. The great amount of pottery at most sites suggested a possible key to their relative chronological placement. The most unique feature of Mesa Verde remained what it had

been in the beginning—the size, fineness, and number of its cliff houses.

The Mesa Verde archaeological program progressed during the 1920s when Jesse L. Nusbaum, a trained archaeologist, served as park superintendent. More intensive surveys added to the total site inventory. Farming terraces behind alignments of stones found on many drainage lines and at least one possible reservoir for water storage afforded ideas of ancient agricultural practices. They were supplemented by an experimental garden planted with native corn to determine necessary amounts of moisture and length of maturation periods. Petroglyph panels, house remains on mesas lying outside the core areas where most efforts had been focused, scattered artifacts, and human burials that had escaped earlier detection were recorded or collected. Repeated occupations of some villages, one on top of another, were confirmed. Pithouses exposed in Step House Cave on Wetherill Mesa were far more primitive than the surface structure there and resembled those opened earlier on Chapin Mesa. In the terminology then used, the former were *Basketmaker,* the latter *Pueblo,* but both were actually aspects of the single Anasazi continuum.

Scientists from Gila Pueblo, a private research center, made potsherd collections in the effort to establish a local developmental sequence for the pottery making craft and detect possible trade connections to other districts. As the decade ended, all this newly gathered data could be used to understand the Anasazi lifestyle of Mesa Verde and the northern Southwest.

ARCHAEOLOGICAL RESEARCH AT MESA VERDE

Mesa Verde has continued to receive close scrutiny by scientists. Because of the public nature of the holding, there has been a dual mission: first, to increase the knowledge of the Anasazi and how they utilized their environment; and second, to make that information available to visitors to the park.

Surveyors have learned by experience to identify the type, probable size and estimated

Dr. Jesse Walter Fewkes in front of Mesa Verde's first "museum," 1916.

age of Mesa Verde's many prehistoric sites. This data has been used to plan excavation programs, and to interpret settlement patterns and population density through time. The rough topography and thick vegetation of Mesa Verde have required repetitious tramping over the same ground to record all the thousands of places the ancients left clues of their passing.

Lightning-ignited forest fires, while not welcomed, have exposed otherwise hidden remains and immediate surveys of burn areas have become routine. A slight depression, a few fire-reddened rocks, soil discoloration, a potsherd or two, fragments of stone tools or projectile points are the only hints of occupation a millenium or more ago. In spite of intensive surveys in and around the park which have identified about 4,000 sites, it is unlikely that

the precise number of sites in this difficult terrain has yet been tabulated.

The bulk of Mesa Verde's Anasazi remains lie buried beneath the earth's surface or the accumulated discards of the past. Controlled sample excavations of all the kinds of sites have been essential to fill gaps in our understanding of the development of the Anasazi culture not visible in the cliff dwellings. Because the early stages were least understood, a dozen pithouse clusters on lower Chapin Mesa have been uncovered. In the same part of the park six surface pueblos representing one or more later occupations have also been cleared. A late masonry village in Soda Canyon was completely excavated. Four surface pueblos and the Mummy Lake reservoir in the Far View group have been studied. Work in Morefield Canyon at

Mesa-top ruins at Far View. Opposite: A ladder access to one of Far View's rooms.

the northeast end of the park includes an excavation of an isolated hilltop kiva, two early-to-middle period villages, a possible reservoir, and two Great Kivas. Sites not used in the interpretive program have been carefully backfilled to protect them from the elements.

Once the cliff dwellings were cleared, it was learned some were threatened by water seeping from beneath their protective sandstone shells or pouring over cliff faces after summer thunderstorms or spring thaws. As tourism burgeoned to hundreds of thousands of visitors annually and more sites on the mesa tops were opened, further destructive elements were recognized. Attrition, moisture, van-

dalism, and even sonic booms have taken their toll. Consequently, a stabilization and repair program has become a permanent part of park activity. Diversion dikes have been erected to direct water away from fragile walls. Roofs have been erected over clay or slab-lined subsurface units; upper courses of masonry in surface and cliff dwellings have been reset in mortar. Because stabilization crews often work side by side with excavators, their interaction has led to further enlightenment about Anasazi construction methods.

Over the years activities related to excavation, preservation, and interpretation have included detailed mapping of major

Nordenskïold's photo of Cliff Palace before excavation.

Excavating Far View ruins, about 1916.

structures, photograph files documenting all aspects of the prehistory and its natural setting, dating through tree-ring sampling from architectural timbers or charcoal recovered from excavations, and preparation of museum displays.

In the beginnings of Mesa Verde research participants learned techniques of excavation and archaeological deduction *in situ* because the discipline was in its infancy. Taking this cue, from 1953 to 1956 the University of Colorado operated a summer field school in Mesa Verde National Park to train students of archaeology in practical application of their campus curriculae. During the 1960s a research center replaced the school but still used and trained student help. A cadre of young professionals

Mesa Verde conference of National Park superintendents and naturalists, 1925.

emerged from these activities, many of whom continue to conduct research in the Southwest.

THE WETHERILL MESA PROJECT

For half a century the antiquities on Wetherill Mesa had been held in reserve while those on Chapin Mesa were exploited for the benefit of both the public and the scientific community. Other than the uncovering of the Basketmaker pithouses in Step House Cave in 1926 and some re-examination of other sites worked over by the Wetherills and Nordenskïold in the late 1800s, no serious excavation had been undertaken. Thus, the mesa was suitable for a

large-scale research endeavor begun in 1958 with financial assistance from the National Geographic Society. Customary in this federal preserve, one goal was to enhance the layman's Mesa Verde National Park experience by adding attractions to be viewed with less congestion. A second goal was to further scientific knowledge through use of the most current technologies.

After five years' work, the results were impressive. A meticulous survey of Wetherill Mesa added over 800 sites to the park's tabulation. Long House, the second largest of all the cliff dwellings, and two other similar but smaller towns, Mug House and Step House, had been cleared. The latter with its early period pithouses has been made ready for

27

A detail of Long House ruin. Opposite: an early Nordenskïold photo of Long House.

viewing. Six mesa top sites extended the span of remains back to the dawn of Mesa Verde prehistory. From all these settlements a wealth of specimens had been obtained. Related ecological, biological, geological and ethnographical studies enriched the record obtained from the ground. Piece by piece the ancient Mesa Verdians were being made more understandable.

In recognition of its outstanding archaeological remains and its importance in preserving the global heritage of mankind, in September, 1978 the United Nations' Educational, Scientific, and Cultural Organization designated Mesa Verde National Park a World Cultural Heritage site.

CHAPTER III

MESA VERDE'S ARCHAEOLOGICAL EVIDENCE

THE HAMLETS, VILLAGES AND CLIFF CITIES OF THE ANASAZI

Anasazi remains abound in Mesa Verde National Park and adjacent parts the Four Corners region. More than 4,000 sites are known within the park itself. Pottery and architectural characteristics indicate changing lifestyles and different responses to natural factors that may be grouped into three developmental stages.

HAMLETS—A.D. 500-900
(Also known as Basketmaker III and Pueblo I)

The lengthy earliest stage of settled life on the Mesa Verde was a formative period when the culture and its tools first developed. It has been the most difficult to learn about. Passing centuries and re-use of some localities by different groups have obliterated obvious signs of dwellings carved out of the ground. Now, a century of research has uncovered interesting details about the lives of early inhabitants.

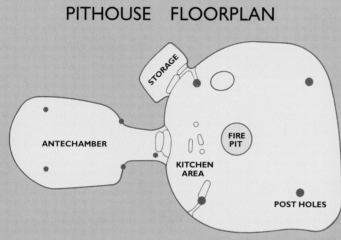

PITHOUSE FLOORPLAN

STORAGE

ANTECHAMBER

FIRE PIT

KITCHEN AREA

POST HOLES

Preceding page: Dr. Douglas Osborne with Wetherill Mesa Project artifacts. Right: viewing an excavated pithouse.

HAMLET ARCHITECTURE

The first occupants took advantage of Mesa Verde's natural landscape features for protection of their rudimentary dwellings fashioned from the dirt, rocks and trees about them. They found sheltered alcoves on cliff escarpments, overhangs along the tops of talus slopes, or in exposed southern mesa tops where wind-deposited soil, or loess, allowed sinking pithouses into the ground. Their structures were designed for single families but were generally clustered in groups of seven or eight forming hamlets of extended family or clan members. Living together in settlements held together by blood ties was a continuation of the nomadic band organization into sedentary life.

The "pits" dished out of the ground comprising each home were circular to squarish, 15 to 20 feet across and 2 to 4 feet deep. A small southern side chamber, a smaller version of the main pithouse, was connected to the main room by a raised passageway. A crude bench, where slanting poles forming the framework of the above-ground walls were sometimes set, encircled most of the pit. The lower part of the bench was occasionally partially lined with vertical stone slabs. On the

A mug from Long House.

An Anasazi cradle board.

floor was a central hearth, storage pits and bins made of stone slabs. In most instances, low, irregular mud-and-stone wing walls partitioned the area adjacent to the antechamber passage from the rest of the living surface. Floor features were stone deflectors to prevent air currents from extinguishing hearth fires and a small hole, or *sipapu,* representing the symbolic entrance to the supernatural world below. Presence of the sipapu suggests that pithouses served both living and ceremonial functions.

Four posts set in a square in the pithouse floor supported four horizontal members, to which were attached angular wall poles and horizontal roof beams. The resulting house, covered in brush and mud, resembled a low truncated cone or pyramid. A roof opening allowed smoke to escape. Often the entrance to the pithouse was an exterior opening in the antechamber. With survival based more on agriculture and group numbers growing, additional storage units were dug into the ground outside the house to bank against the future.

Over several centuries the pithouse concept slowly eroded, so that by A.D. 900 most Mesa Verdians had moved to surface residences for at least part of the year. That shift in residency was one of the most significant changes in Anasazi history. Many elements derived from Anasazi roots survived the shift. Some differences from earlier architecture were in *jacal* walls of posts and mud reinforced with stone chinking, flat pole and mud roofs, and the collection of living and storage units into connected linear plans one or two rooms wide and up to 60 feet long. Hearths, floor bins, and roof smoke holes were retained. So was the old pithouse, which probably continued as a winter residence. As surface living extended year round, the pithouse was converted to a *kiva,* a place for group ritual or social activities.

During the hamlet period, another kind of specialized facility, the *Great Kiva,* appeared in some Mesa Verde communities. Perhaps introduced to the Anasazi by immediate neighbors to the south, it was a larger, circular, subterranean room. Great Kivas are thought to have served the spiritual and social needs of one or more communities. Several ordinary kivas in each hamlet were meeting places for family groups of clans.

HAMLET ARTIFACTS, CRAFTS AND TOOLS

The Anasazi became skilled in the complex technology of converting raw clay to durable earthenware early in their settled history, and the study of this pottery is essential to the archaeological reconstruction of their past. Hamlet-dwelling Mesa Verdians fashioned gray and black-on-white wares from clay found in shale beds exposed along talus slopes of the canyons. They made their pottery with a coiling technique: rings welded together by scraping and smoothing the surfaces. Brief firing of the finished pots in small bonfires made them hard and suitable for many purposes. Some shapes and designs are similar to other kinds of containers, such as gourds or baskets.

The range of pottery forms reflects the makers' simple close-to-the-earth way of life. Kitchen utensils were squat, wide-mouthed jars for cooking over hearthstones or storing dry ingredients until needed. Bowls were communal eating dishes. Large, tall-necked jars with narrow mouths held water dipped from a spring by earthenware ladles. These utilitarian items were undecorated, except for unsmoothed bands on the necks of some jars. Small figurines (probably used in fertility rites) and tubular or elbow-shaped pipes for smoking wild tobacco or other dried plants were also unpainted.

As the period progressed, black to brownish designs produced from plant juice or crushed mineral pigments were painted on some of the gray bowls, pitchers, ladles, high-shouldered jars, and animal form effigies. Some decorating followed naturalistic motifs, but more were geometric.

The presence of a few black-on-red and red-on-orange pots suggests contact with southeastern Utah people, who developed these kinds of ceramics. Tools for pulverizing foods; slabs *(metates)* with troughed grinding surfaces and handstones *(manos);* axes, choppers, and hammers were pecked and ground from the harder sandstones and igneous intrusions of the region. Projectile points for spears and arrows, knives, scrapers and drills were chipped from chert and quartzite found in small quantities in gravel deposits on the mesa, in the Mancos Valley, or imported from more

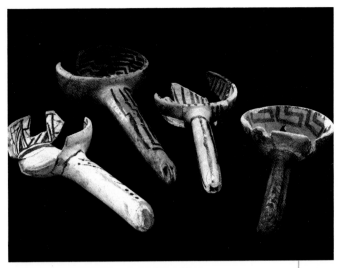

Black-on-white ladles from Mug House.

Corn, grown on the mesa top, was an important part of the Anasazi diet.

VILLAGES — A.D. 900-1075 (Also known as Pueblo II)

EVOLUTION OF PITHOUSE

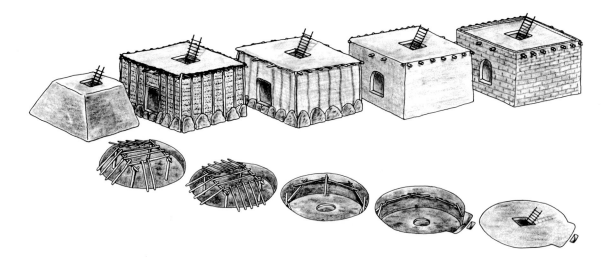

The Basketmaker Period pithouse was developed by the Anasazi into two distinct architectural forms. Pole-and-mud construction, top, led to a roofed pueblo. The "pit" evolved into a subterranean kiva.

More collections of larger surface houses appeared on low ridges of the mesa tops during this 175-year period, though some villagers continued to dwell in caves, on talus slopes and in canyon bottoms.

VILLAGE ARCHITECTURE

Communities were now made up of a single or double row of up to fifteen rectangular, flat-roofed, one-story adjoining rooms. True masonry appeared in house walls. At first, sandstone blocks from nearby exposures, with edges roughly dressed by chipping, were laid up randomly in narrow walls a single stone wide. Later, building stones were better and more uniformly shaped and set in two-stone widths. Some walls were footed upon large upright slabs, more massive than those of earlier times. Interior and exterior wall surfaces were plastered with smoothed mud that washed off outer surfaces rapidly when

untended. Roofs consisted of beams topped by smaller elements of wood and bark over which a thick layer of dirt was spread. Access to houses was either through a roof or side entry. Floors generally had firepits, corner storage enclosures, and milling bins in which flat surfaced metates were permanently seated.

Kivas were sunk into the ground immediately in front of the room block. A ladder protruding from their smokehole entrances in the flat, ground-level roofs announced when they were in use. Masonry lining strengthened the earth wall of the pit. A cribbed roof was supported by four posts or, more commonly, by four or six stone pilasters evenly spaced on the bench. A kiva connected to a circular tower made its first appearance.

Great Kivas were still incorporated into certain settlements. Small field houses, temporarily occupied during growing seasons, were maintained near garden plots.

A tower-to-kiva tunnel at Badger House.

VILLAGE POTTERY

Two innovations in the pottery craft are hallmarks of this period. On the exteriors of most gray vessels, such as jars and pitchers, coils were not obliterated but were carefully pinched between thumb and forefinger to create indentations, called *corrugations* by archaeologists. Some indentations captured the fingerprints of potters, extending a very personal bond across the ages. Occasionally pinch marks were spaced to create neat diagonal patterning. In addition to its aesthetic appeal, this unique roughening of vessel surfaces had the practical advantages of heat retention and reduced slippage—especially important with the huge, bulbous, handleless jars then being made. This corrugation of utilitarian wares continued for the remainder of the Anasazi lifespan.

The second ceramic advancement was the practice of slipping vessels to be decorated. A wash of fine-grained, white firing clay applied before firing created a light unblemished surface over which new types of geometric patterns were painted. During the early phases of the village stage, artisans showed a preference for a distinctive layout of fine-lined designs, combining lines, dots, solid triangles, scrolls and hatchure laid in panels on bowls, jars, pitchers and ladles. Later, bolder patterns featured large triangles, checkerboards and hatchures. These two recognizable successive styles have provided an important means for dating materials. Red and orange pottery, apparently valued by some Mesa Verdians but not made by local potters, continued to be procured from folks living to the west and south.

CHANGES IN VILLAGE LIFE

The established conservatism of the Anasazi rhythm of life meant there were few alterations to the inventory of material goods, though minor modifications improved the

Mummy Lake. Preceding page: daily life in a mesa-top hamlet.

efficiency of some tools. Cotton, woven into coarse textiles, was one new acquisition.

However, significant demographic changes were at hand. More and larger villages appeared, many on marginal agricultural lands in eastern canyons or middle mesas of the park, with sizeable burial grounds amid greater trash accumulation. It would appear that long tillage of the mesa top and increasing numbers of Mesa Verdians needing to be fed forced expansion into less desirable sectors. The resourceful Anasazi responded to what must have been a developing crisis with newly devised water and soil conservation methods. Small check dams and terraces were thrown across drainages to hold both soil and water; catchment ponds and irrigation ditches to channel runoff were dug; reservoirs were constructed. And then surely the Anasazi danced and sang in their kivas praying for rain and snow melt to fill them.

A water collection cove in Spruce Tree Canyon. Opposite, top: Oak Tree House. Opposite, below: museum diorama depicts construction of the pueblos.

TOWNS—A.D. 1075-1300 (Also known as Pueblo III)

Although small settlements continued to be occupied in all the various environmental enclaves found in the park, there was a trend at this time toward fewer, larger, more elaborate towns. Some remained on the mesa tops, but, for unknown reasons, about A.D. 1200 there was a major shift to cliff shelters that impacted daily life as greatly as the earlier move to surface houses. Great towns in both settings were surrounded by lesser satellite communities, and some formerly occupied districts were abandoned. Concentrations of both secular and sacred constructions near these town clusters point to a mixture of economic, political and religious factors.

43

ARCHITECTURE OF MESA VERDE TOWNS

Multiroom, multilevel dwellings accommodating large numbers of individuals and clans and incorporating living, storing, working, socializing and worshipping areas within a well defined space were characteristic of the time. When erected in the open, these towns varied from compact, orderly, rectangular house blocks to more extended linear, L- or U-shaped plans. Living rooms, storerooms, ceremonial chambers, courtyards over kiva roof tops, towers, Great Kivas, or a retaining wall between the town and its dump were principal features.

Irregularities of shape, uneven rock floors, or massive detritus falls in some caves chosen for occupation required modifications of usual town plans, their orientations and certain traditional features. Rigid rectangular plans were generally impossible. Arrangements that molded like putty into nooks and crannies but included all the various elements customary in a Mesa Verde Anasazi town took their place. Rooms were generally smaller or more oddly shaped than usual, and narrowed doorways sometimes featured a T-shaped opening. With the support of the rock shelter walls, rooms could be stacked higher, some up to four stories. Their protected location required less substantial construction. Some kivas could not be gouged into hard rock and were built into the domiciliary blocks so as to appear subterranean; their sipapus were either eliminated or opened into walls. In several cases Great Kiva features were placed in courtyards.

Pressure to reside in the cliffs was evidently great. A half dozen of these buildings contained three or four times more rooms than any contemporary surface house yet excavated. Cliff Palace on Chapin Mesa (217 rooms) and Long House on Wetherill Mesa (150 rooms) were the largest two examples. However, the apparent need to make use of every reachable ledge made frequent building of units of six to eight rooms necessary. The sheltered environment of both large and small sites helped preserve some wall plaster, on occasion displaying painted depictions of small creatures who shared the mesa, the imprints of human hands, or geometrics. There were also frequent incised or painted rock art motifs on exposed cliff surfaces.

45

Preceding page: a winter view of Spruce Tree House. Opposite: detail of Cliff Palace. Above: pictographs often decorated interior walls of the cliff dwellings. Right: an Anasazi jar.

ARTS AND CRAFTS OF THE CLIFF CITIES

Whereas the decorative format of earlier ceramics was shared by Anasazi in other regions, during the eleventh through the thirteenth centuries a distinctive Mesa Verdian school of pottery design developed. Using a pigment extracted from plant juices over a highly polished, creamy white surface, carefully drafted, standardized geometric elements were painted. Two forms unique to these potters were handled mugs and a squat vessel with flange and lid called a kiva jar. Wide, heavy-walled bowls still dominated the output of decorated earthenwares.

Gray utility vessels, primarily bell- or egg-shaped jars of several sizes, were uniformly corrugated. Rare incising or attached clay pellets further enhanced the surfaces. Most other durable goods of the town dwellers were identical to those of the hamlet dwellers a half millenium before them. The same continuity of perishables is suggested by finds in the arid caves from both initial and final Mesa Verdian occupation. The amount of these items recovered from the cliff towns was, of course, far greater and included yucca fiber baskets, matting, pot rests, cordage, sandals, pouches and blankets; cotton textiles; wooden household and garden tools; and leather moccasins and pieces of hide.

Beside man-made objects, some of the people themselves were found buried in piles of dry trash or beneath house floors. Under certain circumstances, they had slowly withered to become naturally mummified. Victims of disease, accidents, unsanitary conditions and an uncompromising existence, most of the adults had lived less than four decades on the evergreen Mesa Verde.

ANASAZI LIFE ON THE MESA VERDE

The first Anasazi on the Mesa Verde were dependent upon farming, supplemented by hunting and gathering. Why did they choose this seemingly dubious place to settle? The surrounding valleys offered sources of permanent water and expanses of relatively flat, easily cleared, arable land without the difficulties of deep canyons, perpendicular cliffs and high elevation. Why did they choose the mesa as their home?

In the beginning, cliff alcoves of branching canyons and overhangs along the tops of talus slopes attracted the incoming Anasazi migrating up from Mancos Canyon to the south. These were the kinds of places where their immediate forebears had lived. Later, the Anasazi slowly expanded up to the tops of southern fingers of the mesa, where they could build the same sort of subsurface shelters as in the caves. They stayed for the next four or five centuries while other Anasazi settled in the neighboring valleys and plateaus with comparable conditions.

Studies of tree-rings, plant pollen, and plant and animal remains show the prehistoric Mesa Verde environment was suitable for human occupancy. Water for domestic use was available in seeps and springs where the sandstone met underlying shale. Large and small game was plentiful, as was a variety of wild plants to supplement the diet. There were abundant natural resources for construction, fuel and various technologies. Essential to successful agriculture was the fertile soil blown up out of the deserts to the south and—over geologic time—deposited as a mantle on the sandstone that capped the mesa. Also there was a reasonably dependable annual precipitation from summer rains and winter snows averaging 14 to 18 inches. A long frost-free period of 160 to 170 days and moderately hot summers meant an adequate growing season. Modern measurements that likely duplicate former conditions show that the mesa top is 10° cooler in summer and 10° to 20° warmer in winter than the valleys below.

The Anasazi who came to the Mesa Verde did not live in a vacuum, but were in touch with their fellow Anasazi across the Colorado Plateau. Architectural and ceramic idiosyncracies and trade goods not available locally, such as cotton, turquoise or sea shells, demonstrate this contact.

Mesa Verdians, like other Anasazi, lived together in extended families. Shared labors, resources and mutual support offered protection from the outside world. The success of the agricultural revolution and the absence of warfare promoted population growth. As a result, the groups dwelling together grew, but Anasazi social organization remained unchanged. Relatives or groups of relatives built their pueblos and worked the fields together. Inevitably such communism curbed individual behavior. Conformity was a virtue; deviation was intolerable. This spawned a conservatism that can be seen in material goods that remained constant for centuries and a social passivity that forestalled advancement beyond a Stone Age level.

Social and spiritual leaders may have emerged, but archaeology does not indicate that any persons possessed status symbols, such as more lavish living quarters or finer accoutrements. There must have been specializations of labor between individuals and between sexes, but there was no body of full time artisans.

Above: decorated pottery. Opposite: the Anasazi probably performed ceremonies in the kivas and village plazas.

The smoke-blackened ceiling of Spruce Tree House's alcove.

The Mesa Verdians arrived with religious orientation and a set of charms revolving about the natural forces that molded their environment. The religious and mundane aspects of Anasazi life were thoroughly intertwined, as shown by sipapus in pithouse floors and the later incorporation of ceremonial chambers into room blocks. As kiva features and orientation became stereotyped, the rituals performed in them may have become conventionalized as well. What is certain is that as conditions of life deteriorated in the thirteenth century, religious fervor mounted. The large cliff dwellings had a ratio of one kiva to every seven to nine dwelling rooms. At times the canyon must have reverberated with chants and the throb of dancing feet.

During the more than seven centuries of Anasazi presence on the Mesa Verde, there was a perceptible ebb and flow of occupation across what is now Mesa Verde National Park.

Hamlets were concentrated on the lower, southernmost sectors of the several secondary mesas in the western part of the park, with garden plots nearby. The remainder of the uplift remained untamed virgin ground appearing much as it does today. For 400 years there was no appreciable outward expansion beyond the strip of land originally claimed.

The village stage commencing about A.D. 900 instigated the greatest distribution of the Mesa Verde Anasazi. By the end of this phase near A.D. 1075 most of the usable areas of the park were occupied. One expansion was up the mesas to higher, less promising districts. Another was into broad canyon bottoms to the east. Exposed mesa tops were used extensively in summer and protected canyon declivities served some of the population as winter grounds. In both instances it was necessary to increase the extent of farm land and water reserves by simple engineering efforts. The

A diorama view of kiva construction.

landscape was further modified by wholesale clearing as more and more plots were brought under cultivation. This widely dispersed settlement pattern endured only about 175 years. The primary reason for rejecting it probably hinged on greater exploitation of less rich soils.

About the late eleventh century another significant demographic adjustment occurred as the people withdrew from much of the eastern reaches of the park to regroup into larger towns on the central ridges of the western mesas. Whatever caused this change, the solution was not permanent. Within little more that a century, another movement took some of the Anasazi over the cliffs to the vaulted alcoves where their Mesa Verde drama had begun. Some even left the mesa to settle with neighbors along and south of the San Juan River. With reduced fuel reserves, the move to the cliffs may have been prompted by a desire for

warmer winter quarters. If so, the Anasazi must have been disappointed, because doubtlessly they found the caves cold, dank, sunless and unhealthy. More likely, lower crop yields meant the farmers needed to open greater patches of mesa top for cultivation. Regardless, that desperate move to the cliffs was also doomed. Within sixty or seventy years most of the cliff dwellers apparently decided life on the Mesa Verde was no longer tenable.

Reasons for ultimate abandonment of this homeland unquestionably were many and cut across environmental, social and religious spheres. The settlements erected in the cliffs with such tremendous effort appear to be those of a threatened people, and the fulfillment of that threat drove them out. The caves were vulnerable to siege, but the archaeological record contains no sign of destruction, fire, or loss of life from strife. Human enemies were apparently not the menace.

CHAPIN MESA
SITES

TO FAR VIEW
VISITOR CENTER
& LODGE

CHAPIN CANYON

SODA CANYON

SPRUCE CANYON

PICNIC
AREA

PARK
HEADQUARTERS

MUSEUM

RUINS ROAD

SPRUCE
TREE
HOUSE

MESA TOP LOOP

CLIFF PALACE LOOP

CHAPIN MESA

NAVAJO CANYON

1 PITHOUSE

VIEW

2
SQUARE
TOWER
HOUSE

3

5
4
PITHOUSES &
PUEBLO RUINS

6

7
PUEBLO
RUINS

8
PUEBLO
RUINS

VIEW
11

SUN
TEMPLE

VIEW 10

SUNPOINT

9
VIEW

12

VIEW
CLIFF
PALACE

VIEW

VIEW

VIEW

BALCONY
HOUSE

CLIFF CANYON

■ MESA TOP RUIN
▲ CLIFF DWELLING
● VIEW

Cliff Palace in winter

of such dwellings in the immediate vicinity. What is seen today is merely a large, shallow, roughly circular unlined pit in the earth, where perhaps a single Anasazi family came to terms with a demanding life. When occupied, a crude pole, brush and mud superstructure raised on four upright posts only several feet above ground level served as roof. Analysis of annual growth rings remaining in chunks of charcoal recovered from the pithouse suggests the possibility that this roof burned about A.D. 575.

Interior pithouse features were a stone-ringed firepit and floor cists for storage of foodstuffs or valuables. Cooking, eating and sleeping took place on fiber mats on the ground. In spite of its rudimentary nature, this sort of subsurface dwelling was a major advancement over life without shelter. Though dark, it was snug during the severe winters at this almost 7,000 foot elevation. The ground provided insulation and combined body heat fended off the numbing cold. It must have nourished a close psychological attachment to the womb of the earth, from which the idea of the subterranean religious center, the kiva, may have evolved.

Stop 2: Observe here the dramatic 700-foot deep Navajo Canyon slicing back into the Mesa Verde for fifteen miles and the capping of Cliff House sandstone. Over millions of years water seeping down into the porous sandstone and emerging on cliff faces caused spalling, and created the alcoves where thirteenth century Mesa Verdians erected their final communal homes. More than 60 such structures are situated in eroded recesses along Navajo Canyon, many of them containing a half dozen or fewer rooms. One called Echo House, with 20 rooms and 2 kivas, can be seen directly across the canyon from this point. Located on the tour route immediately after the earliest type of pithouse, it vividly demonstrates 700 years of architectural advancement.

Stop 3: Square Tower House, discovered in 1888 from the mesa edge near Stop 3 and repaired in 1919, is what remains of a 13th century 80-room structure that rose to four stories in some portions against the supporting cliff wall. It is an example of the town stage of the Southwest Tradition. In this case, the so-called tower is actually the remnant of a

Navajo Canyon. Opposite: Square Tower House.

larger multistoried house unit. Considerable timber has survived in this building, including two partial kiva roofs.

Since this settlement was reached from above and below only by shallow hand and toe hold trails—worn by hammerstones pecking relentlessly against the cliff face—the determination, agility, balance and outright derring-do displayed by the Anasazi is astounding. All building materials for Square Tower House, raw resources for handicrafts, foodstuffs and water had to be either transported up or down the sheer escarpment on human backs, or raised and lowered by teams of men with ropes. Without pulleys or hoists, there was no substitute for muscle; and without surefootedness there was no tomorrow.

Stops 4, 5, 6: Three distinct occupations spanning three centuries, from about A.D. 675 to 950, have been exposed here. During these years the Mesa Verdians came out of the ground to dwell on the surface, while remaining essentially in the same locale.

The first dwellers continued to live in one-room pithouses, of which two consecutive examples are present. One intrudes on the remains of the other. The pithouse had become larger and deeper than at Stop 1 and was outfitted with several innovations, such as a vertical ventilator shaft to improve domestic air quality and a low earthen bench around perimeters which may have served as a sleeping platform.

Nearby is evidence for a later semisubterranean phase, where the Anasazi showed themselves to be slowly rejecting the pithouse and moving toward the village stage of the Southwest Tradition. Shallow slab-lined rooms were squared. It is known from other such sites that above-ground walls were of upright poles separated by intertwined branches, plastered together with large amounts of mud (wattle-and-daub), and flat roofs were formed by beams covered with brush and more mud. A single row of such *jacal* rooms adjoined each other in an arc-shaped ground plan.

A mesa-top kiva, showing details of construction.

Farther down the path are the remains—no more than rocks laid in a rectangular pattern—of a tenth century village. By that time, connected living rooms of unshaped stone blocks set in mud mortar had replaced the earlier flimsy *jacale* structures and the old pithouse had become a place of worship. Roof support columns of the pithouse-turned-kiva were stone, but otherwise it retained characteristics of the earthen pit domicile from the preceding half millenium. Literally and figuratively, the Anasazi remained rooted to Mother Earth and would continue to be throughout their later history.

Stop 7: This stop presents further evidence of a site used for a number of generations. The first post-and-mud early Pueblo village here, likely dating in the ninth century, was destroyed by a fire that left only charred stubs of supporting wall members. A second occupation came about A.D. 1000 when a few adjoining surface rooms were built of single courses of roughly shaped stones laid in thick mud mortar. A more advanced subterranean kiva with masonry facing on the bench shows increased formality in orientation. The final structure, yielding a tree-ring date of A.D. 1074, was a larger but more compact pueblo with walls of double-coursed masonry built over the second village. New characteristics included several towers incorporated into or beside the building mass.

Stop 8: Sun Point Pueblo, a 30-room enclosed structure surrounding a kiva connected by an underground tunnel to a tower, illustrates the last Anasazi residency on the mesa top. It was occupied about A.D. 1200 and was a full-fledged masonry pueblo of the culminating town stage of the Southwest Tradition. Although its appearance is defensive,

Sun Temple.

evidence of conflict is lacking. Masons erecting 10 cliff-side houses visible in the vicinity seem to have robbed this briefly-occupied town of its building stones and timbers.

Stop 9: One of the most impressive observation places in the park is Sun Point, overlooking the juncture of Cliff and Fewkes Canyons. About 100 feet below the mesa crust is a concentration of thirteenth century cliff dwellings—including Mesa Verde's centerpiece, Cliff Palace. Most are in shadow until afternoon, but in any light their coloration and lines were natural camouflauge. On a mesa top rim to the left is the unique Sun Temple.

Stop 10: From this point on the south rim of Fewkes Canyon Oak Tree House, with 50 rooms and 6 kivas, can be viewed on the opposite cliff.

Stop 11: This stop provides good views of Fire Temple and New Fire House near the head of Fewkes Canyon, both named for their similarities to Hopi ceremonial chambers. Fire Temple, unusual in having a central dance plaza with Great Kiva characteristics, appears to have been strictly ceremonial. Fire Temple is known for the colored naturalistic and geometric painted motifs on its walls.

Stop 12: The Mesa Top Loop doubles back a short distance to the last site of the route, Sun Temple. The purpose of this oddly-shaped enclosed structure with its series of massive, rubble-filled walls forming narrow side chambers around a double courtyard and three circular kiva-like units is unknown. Its careful—though unfinished—masonry, commanding placement and unique features suggest a religious function. Another view of Cliff Palace on the opposite side of Cliff Canyon can be enjoyed from here—the point from which the ruin was first seen by white men.

Left: Cliff Palace. Above: a common raven.

CLIFF PALACE LOOP The left hand one-way road off the Ruins Road runs along the top of an arm of Chapin Mesa separated by Cliff and Soda canyons. A ten minute drive brings park visitors to the spectacle most come to see: the awe-inspiring Cliff Palace.

A short trail from the parking area leads to a projecting cliff edge on the north side of the village for an almost aerial perspective of the plan and orientation of Cliff Palace. In the huge (89 feet deep and 59 feet high) overhang is the largest of Mesa Verde's cliff dwellings. Access to the dwelling today involves a steep, winding path and four 10-foot ladders which were not available to the ancients. Visitors are restricted to the narrow artificial terrace in front of the building that was once the trash heap where discards—and the dead—were placed. Above it rise 217 rooms, stacked in tiers up to four stories, over an uneven alcove floor made level with fill behind a retaining wall.

An enormous chunk of cliff rock too ponderous for the Anasazi to move had been braced with masonry in hopes it would not shift and take part of the town with it. The shape of the cave made Cliff Palace's compact rooms and irregular village plan necessary. Some interior rooms still contain decorative paintings done in earthy pigments.

Not all rooms were built at one time. As needs changed, this and other pueblos were

Views of Cliff Palace.

constantly growing or retracting. Signs of remodeling are numerous. A series of 14 storage rooms crammed onto a narrow ledge above the dwellings appear unreachable, but in ancient times they could be entered from roofs now collapsed.

The 23 kivas in Cliff Palace, used by clans making up the community, show the final development of this architectural form at Mesa Verde. Kivas were usually built up with fill around the outer walls, making them appear subterranean. The kiva featured a deflector to keep incoming air passing down the ventilator shaft from extinguishing firepit flames directly behind it. A sipapu, or symbolic floor hole to the spirit world, was located behind the firepit. Many were aligned south-north in front of what had become a characteristic recess in the southern section of the masonry-lined kiva wall. A hatchway in the low, cribbed roof—stout enough to support traffic—was still the entrance. Occasional side doorways to tunnels must have allowed ceremony participants to

make dramatic, unanticipated entrances.

Wood taken from the ruin dated between A.D. 1209 and the 1270s, after which construction ceased.

In 1909 most of Cliff Palace was made secure for future visitors. By then it had been stripped of its portable riches by treasure hunters, who had camped for weeks at a time within its rubble. The tallest tower and the large boulder later were reinforced. The inherent beauty of the old house, enhanced by the caressing patina of time and the care of the National Park Service stabilization crews, make it the most photographed prehistoric monument in the United States.

Stop 2: Balcony House, the first of the major "lost cities" of the Mesa Verde to be rediscovered by Americans, is a rare experience for visitors. It cannot be seen from the Cliff Palace Loop road nor any overlook except one on a trail a short distance beyond the car stop. Out of view, it sits in a high cave on the east side of this projection of Chapin Mesa,

facing down Soda Canyon. Here modern viewers have a taste of Anasazi cliff-side stamina and daring, even though the hand and toe holds of the Mesa Verdians have been replaced with a 32-foot ladder to reach the house and a return crawlhole and strenuous but safe climb back up the cliff. This is no place for the faint of heart, but those who make the effort to tour the site will be amply rewarded. Standing in the courtyard looking down the heights brings a heady exhilaration and deep appreciation for the demanding lifestyle of the former inhabitants.

CEDAR TREE TOWER Driving north up Chapin Mesa from the museum area, a short side road to the right leads to a late Anasazi site, Cedar Tree Tower, perched on the cliff edge with a panoramic view down Soda Canyon. The expertly constructed two-story tower is connected to a subterranean kiva by an underground tunnel. Since there are no associated dwellings or trash deposits, it is assumed that Cedar Tree Tower was a joint-use ceremonial site for the Anasazi villages in the vicinity.

There are 57 towers in the park, but their precise role in the Anasazi pattern of life is uncertain. Those related to kivas likely provided ceremony participants an opportunity for dramatic entrance. However, some towers are isolated. They may have been lookouts for either peaceful or defensive purposes. Perhaps they were an integral part of a signaling network linking villages. Or they may have been used for making astronomical observations vital to the seasonal planting, harvesting and ritual cycles. The present thick vegetation was likely reduced in aboriginal times by farm clearings, but there are so few elevations above prevailing ground level that general visibility still would have been only a few hundred yards. Since occupied mesas were separated by deep sheer-walled canyons, contact between groups must have been greatly hampered.

Below Cedar Tree Tower are a few artificial terraces of soil built up behind lines of rocks laid across a drainage line. This common Mesa Verdian method increased garden plots in places likely to catch runoff water. Hundreds of such terraces and check dams have been tabulated in Mesa Verde National Park.

FAR VIEW The Far View cluster of villages lies about a mile south of the commercial complex and Visitor Center named for it. Best illustrating the late pueblo-housed, agriculturally-based Mesa Verde occupation, the six sites open for viewing are east of the road down Chapin Mesa and within easy walking distance of a parking area.

1916 Jesse W. Fewkes of the Smithsonian Institution excavated the first mesa top site here. Far View House is the largest structure, originally on two levels, with 40 to 50 rooms and 5 kivas. Built over trash of an earlier occupation, this building dates from the last two centuries the Anasazi lived on Mesa Verde (A.D. 1100 to 1300). This well-organized quadrangle of spacious rooms with relatively large doorways contrasts sharply to the tight, twisting plans of the cliff homes.

To the south is the smaller, enclosed Pipe Shrine House, also built over an earlier surface structure. A number of clay pipes used in ceremonies were recovered from a kiva here.

Far View Tower, northwest of the large house, is a two-story tower with 16 adjacent rooms and 2 kivas, one of which was remodeled from an earlier version. A previous village of single-coursed masonry lies underneath. A nearby burial ground was associated with one or both villages.

Still farther northward is Megalithic House, a complex of 7 rooms and a kiva. Huge boulders are set around the bases of two rooms in a style probably retained from the earliest surface pueblos on lower Chapin Mesa, where slab-lined, shallow, semisubterranean rooms were characteristic. The fact that the other five rooms were of single-course masonry suggests Megalithic House is a survivor from the first phase in the Far View locality, perhaps during the 10th century.

A fifth village, site 820, to the south of the entrance road was another compact rectangular unit of 34 double-coursed rooms, 4 kivas and a tower. It was lived in for a century between A.D. 1050 and 1150 and, like its neighbors, was on ground used by predecessors.

Three sites excavated and backfilled on the mesa top to the west of the road, and nearly 50 other structures within a half square mile, show middle Chapin Mesa was the most densely occupied sector of the park for the 350

Preceding page: a ruin adjacent to Cliff Palace. Left: Far View Ruin. Above: adjoining rooms at Far View.

years between the early pithouses and the later cliff dwellings on the lower mesa. Perhaps as many as 500 people lived on this part of the mesa.

The short growing season at this 7,600-foot elevation, the thin soil and the absence of a permanent watercourse meant a technology was needed to sustain such a large population. Nothing illustrated Mesa Verdians' ingenious adaptation to the environment so well as their elaborate water control system. Mummy Lake reservoir, a key part of this system, is open for viewing in the Far View complex.

Middle Chapin Mesa receives an average 18 inches of annual precipitation, but greater amounts fall on higher ground to the north. Southward sloping channels dug in the vicinity of the Far View cafeteria and service station led into a ditch funneling runoff water a half mile

Walls of Far View Ruin under snow.

down to the intake of the masonry-lined, 90-foot wide reservoir. The angle of the intake channel was engineered to allow silt to settle before the water reached the basin, where it was stored, clear of sediments, for domestic use. Ditches cutting off the main channel are believed to have taken other water to fields.

Although the Mummy Lake water system was the most elaborate, other reservoirs have been found on Mesa Verde. Centuries of construction and maintenance of the water control network demonstrate the Anasazi's practical intelligence and social cooperation.

WETHERILL MESA A 12-mile scenic drive takes off near the Far View Visitor Center for the western plateaus of the park. Enroute there is a series of turnouts where one can view the Montezuma Valley, several distant Anasazi structures and displays giving information about the area's geology, natural history and

prehistory. Of particular interest is an extensive area that still retains scars from a disastrous fire ignited by a lightning strike in the summer of 1934.

STEP HOUSE Reached on foot from the parking area at the end of the Wetherill Mesa entrance road, the Step House cave contains ruins of both the earliest and latest Mesa Verde habitations—separated by 600 years. Many of the alcoves along the canyon walls had probably witnessed similar repeated occupation, but in other instances later remains completely obscured evidence of previous use except for early artifacts recovered among cliff dwelling discards.

In 1891 Nordenskïold dug at Step House and suspected the two distinct occupations. He confined his work to the classic thirteenth century cliff house. In 1926 a hamlet stage pithouse village of four or five units, dated

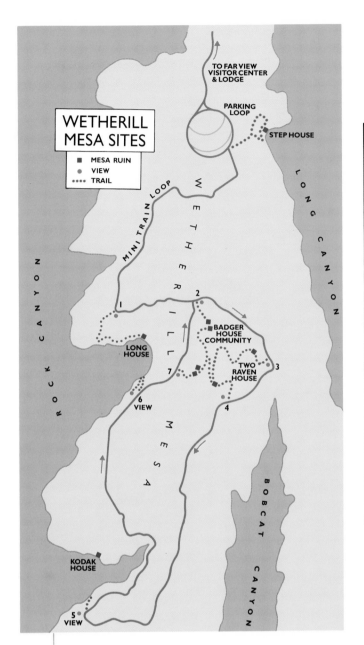

WETHERILL MESA SITES

- ■ MESA RUIN
- ● VIEW
- •••• TRAIL

TO FAR VIEW
VISITOR CENTER
& LODGE

PARKING
LOOP

STEP HOUSE

MINI TRAIN LOOP

WETHERILL

LONG CANYON

ROCK CANYON

1

2

BADGER
HOUSE
COMMUNITY

LONG
HOUSE

7

TWO
RAVEN
HOUSE

3

6
VIEW

4

MESA

BOBCAT CANYON

KODAK
HOUSE

5
VIEW

One of Mesa Verde's wild turkeys.

approximately A.D. 626, was excavated in the southern part of the alcove near rows of large rocks arranged up a slope in a "step" fashion. Both dwellings are now presented, side by side, for park visitors to view.

A multistoried masonry grouping with the usual kiva, storage and work areas attest that the latest town stage Mesa Verdians lived at Step House. Their town was built in the opposite end of the overhang, although all traces of the pithouses probably had been obliterated at that time. In one area of Step House more than 1,600 corn cobs and seeds of ten different wild plants were recovered from the drifted fill dirt. This cache was part of the food supply for the 40 to 50 individuals who once called Step House home.

MINI-TRAIN LOOP

Ruins on lower Wetherill Mesa are reached by a free mini-train departing from the parking lot at brief intervals. Three stops are at ruin groups, two are at overlooks of cliff dwellings, and others are for purposes of boarding or leaving the train.

Stop 1—Long House: Ranger-guided tours of Long House depart from the first stop. Second-largest of Mesa Verde's cliff dwellings, with 150 rooms and 21 kivas, Long House was explored in the late ninteenth century by the Wetherills, Nordenskïold and others. As at Cliff

73

Preceding page: Long House. Above: excavated Two Raven House.

Palace, a series of rooms on a high—now inaccessible—ledge were for storage. Excavations undertaken in the late 1950s and early 1960s recovered many artifacts not found by the 19th century collectors, including blankets, pottery, implements and jewelry. Twenty-eight burials were taken from the refuse. Named for the unusual length of its overhang, Long House featured a plaza in the foreground with several recessed pits, or floor vaults, similar to those in Great Kivas. Perhaps community ceremonies took place in this plaza, with spectators seated on benches and terraces of the house structure.

Stop 2: The Badger House Community sequence of mesa top sites spans the total Anasazi occupation of the Mesa Verde. Located here are a pithouse and an arc-shaped pole-and-mud surface structure of the hamlet stage, as well as successive, more complex masonry rooms, kivas and towers of the village and town stage occupations. Their setting on the

broadest part of Wetherill Mesa; their evolutionary progression; and the artifacts they yielded conform to the Chapin Mesa patterns.

Although the Badger House sites are self-guiding, a National Park Service ranger is present to further interpret the archaeological evidence.

Stop 3: Two Raven House, reached by a self-guiding trail, is a small masonry-walled settlement built over the remains of an earlier pole-brush-mud structure. The exhibited unit consists of ten rooms, a kiva and a pit room. It was inhabited between A.D. 1030 and 1100 during the village stage of Mesa Verde's history. Lines of post holes suggest the settlement may have been encircled by a wooden stockade.

Stop 5 overlooks Kodak House, a 60-room building named by Nordenskïold, who hid his camera there when it was not being used. **Stop 6** affords a view of Long House. Both offer excellent photographic opportunities.

Anasazi art, highlight of the Petroglyph Point Trail.

MESA VERDE ON FOOT Because of the fragile nature of the antiquities in Mesa Verde National Park, hiking is restricted to six day-use trails from which the natural setting can be experienced. Backpacking and cross country trekking are not permitted.

Petroglyph Point Trail, 2.8 miles in length, takes off from the Spruce Tree House trail to the east of the museum. It goes in a southerly direction along the mesa edge and ascends 100 feet to the mesa ridge, where a clear view of Spruce and Navajo canyons can be seen. A panel of petroglyphs is visible on a cliff face just before the trail ascends. The trail returns along the mesa top to the parking area near headquarters.

The Spruce Canyon Trail is a 2.1-mile loop starting at Spruce Tree House and ending in the picnic ground. It descends 500 feet to the canyon bottom, rounds a point, and then proceeds up Spruce Canyon. The change in flora and temperature from mesa top to canyon floor makes this an interesting, though somewhat strenuous, hike. In late afternoon flocks of buzzards circle overhead, riding the air currents before roosting in tall trees or cliff rock.

Register at park headquarters before hiking either the Petroglyph Point or Spruce Canyon trails. Maps and trail guides are available at the museum bookshop. Remember that the Archaeological Resources Protection Act of 1979 prohibits the defacing or removal of any object of antiquity within the park, offenses punishable by fines or imprisonment.

Point Lookout Trail, a 2.3-mile trail in the Morefield Campground area, traverses the south side of the promontory dominating the park entrance and then follows the mesa to viewpoints toward Montezuma and Mancos valleys 2,000 feet below.

Above: foliage of the Gambel Oak.
Opposite: Knife Edge. Inset: mule deer.

Knife Edge Trail, 1.5 miles, leaves the northwest corner of the campground to follow an abandoned road along the north mesa slope known as the Knife Edge to the Montezuma Valley Overlook. With an unobstructed western exposure, the sunset views from here can be spectacular.

Prater Ridge Trail, the longest in the park at 7.8 miles, ascends the east side of Prater Ridge from the campground, goes around the top of the ridge, and returns to the campground by the same route. It affords magnificent distant vistas and enjoyment of the flora and fauna typical of the park.

The **Wetherill Nature Trail** explores the mesa top near the Wetherill Mesa parking area. A National Park Service brochure identifies the flora featured on this short, peaceful walk.

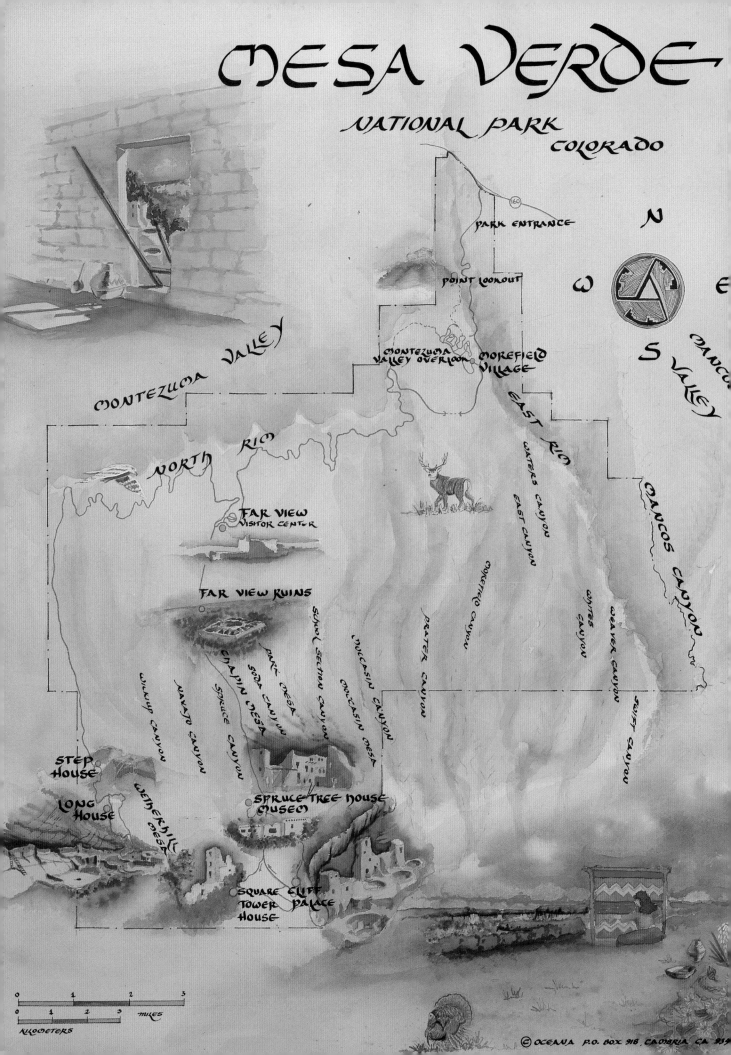

MESA VERDE

NATIONAL PARK

COLORADO

PARK ENTRANCE

POINT LOOKOUT

MONTEZUMA VALLEY OVERLOOK

MOREFIELD VILLAGE

MONTEZUMA VALLEY

NORTH RIM

EAST RIM

FAR VIEW
VISITOR CENTER

FAR VIEW RUINS

SCHOOL SECTION CANYON

PARK MESA

SODA CANYON

CHAPIN MESA

SPRUCE CANYON

NAVAJO CANYON

WICKIUP CANYON

WETHERILL MESA

STEP
HOUSE

LONG
HOUSE

MOCCASIN MESA

MOCCASIN CANYON

PRATER CANYON

MOREFIELD CANYON

EAST CANYON

WATERS CANYON

WHITES CANYON

WEAVER CANYON

SWIFT CANYON

MANCOS CANYON

MANCOS VALLEY

SPRUCE TREE HOUSE
MUSEUM

SQUARE
TOWER
HOUSE

CLIFF
PALACE

STEP
HOUSE

N
W   E
S

160

MILES
0 1 2 3

KILOMETERS
0 1 2 3

© OCEANA P.O. BOX 918, CAMBRIA, CA 934